STATE PROFILES

NEW HAMPSHIRE

BY COLLEEN SEXTON

BELLWETHER MEDIA • MINNEAPOLIS, MN

Blastoff! Discovery launches a new mission: reading to learn. Filled with facts and features, each book offers you an exciting new world to explore!

BLASTOFF! UNIVERSE

BLASTOFF! Beginners — GRADE K

BLASTOFF! READERS — GRADES 1-3

BLASTOFF! DISCOVERY — GRADE 4

This edition first published in 2022 by Bellwether Media, Inc.

No part of this publication may be reproduced in whole or in part without written permission of the publisher.
For information regarding permission, write to Bellwether Media, Inc., Attention: Permissions Department,
6012 Blue Circle Drive, Minnetonka, MN 55343.

Library of Congress Cataloging-in-Publication Data

Names: Sexton, Colleen A., 1967- author.
Title: New Hampshire / by Colleen Sexton.
Description: Minneapolis, MN : Bellwether Media, Inc., 2022. |
    Series: Blastoff! Discovery: State profiles | Includes bibliographical
    references and index. | Audience: Ages 7-13 | Audience: Grades
    4-6 | Summary: "Engaging images accompany information about
    New Hampshire. The combination of high-interest subject matter and
    narrative text is intended for students in grades 3 through 8"–
    Provided by publisher.
Identifiers: LCCN 2021020882 (print) | LCCN 2021020883
    (ebook) | ISBN 9781644873342 (library binding) | ISBN
    9781648341779 (ebook)
Subjects: LCSH: New Hampshire–Juvenile literature.
Classification: LCC F34.3 .S48 2022 (print) | LCC F34.3 (ebook)
    | DDC 974.2–dc23
LC record available at https://lccn.loc.gov/2021020882
LC ebook record available at https://lccn.loc.gov/2021020883

Editor: Rebecca Sabelko   Designer: Brittany McIntosh

Printed in the United States of America, North Mankato, MN.

TABLE OF CONTENTS

FLUME GORGE TRAIL

A family arrives at Franconia Notch State Park on a crisp fall day. They begin their adventure with a hike at the Flume **Gorge** trail. Water spills between rock walls that rise as high as 90 feet (27 meters)!

CURRIER MUSEUM OF ART

HAMPTON BEACH STATE PARK

MOUNT WASHINGTON COG RAILWAY

STRAWBERY BANKE MUSEUM

A FAMOUS FACE

Cannon Mountain once featured a rock formation shaped like a man's face. It was known as the Old Man of the Mountain. This landmark crumbled in 2003.

Later, the family heads to Echo Lake. They watch hawks soar overhead as they paddle kayaks across the clear water. The family ends their day with a tram ride to the top of Cannon Mountain. Fall colors blaze red, orange, and yellow in the forest-covered valleys and nearby mountains. Welcome to New Hampshire!

New Hampshire is part of **New England** in the northeastern United States. Maine borders New Hampshire to the east. The Atlantic Ocean washes the southeastern corner of the state. Massachusetts is New Hampshire's southern neighbor. The Connecticut River forms its western boundary with Vermont. Canada lies across New Hampshire's short northern border.

This triangle-shaped state covers 9,349 square miles (24,214 square kilometers). The capital city of Concord sits in south-central New Hampshire. Manchester, the largest city, lies farther south. Other large cities include Derry and Nashua.

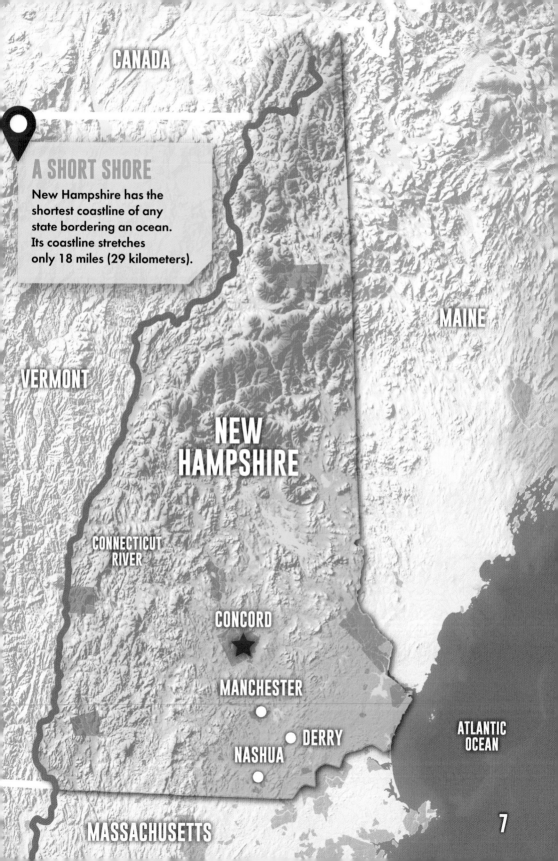

CANADA

A SHORT SHORE

New Hampshire has the shortest coastline of any state bordering an ocean. Its coastline stretches only 18 miles (29 kilometers).

MAINE

VERMONT

NEW HAMPSHIRE

CONNECTICUT RIVER

CONCORD

MANCHESTER

DERRY

NASHUA

ATLANTIC OCEAN

MASSACHUSETTS

WIGWAM

People first arrived in New Hampshire about 12,000 years ago. Over time, Native American groups formed. The largest were the Abenaki. They were hunters and farmers. Many lived in **wigwam** villages along rivers and lakes.

European explorers reached New Hampshire in the early 1600s. The English **settled** around the Piscataqua River in the 1620s. They traded timber, fish, and furs. New Hampshirites fought for their independence in the **Revolutionary War**. New Hampshire became the ninth state in 1788.

NATIVE PEOPLES OF NEW HAMPSHIRE

New Hampshire has no federally recognized tribes in the state today. However, some Native Americans still live throughout the state.

PENNACOOK

- Original lands in southern Maine, northeastern Massachusetts, southern and central New Hampshire, and Vermont
- Moved to Canada in the 1600s due to war and deaths from diseases brought by Europeans
- Some descendants live on two Abenaki reservations in Québec, Canada, today
- Also called Pawtucket and Merrimack

WESTERN ABENAKI

- Original lands in New Hampshire and Vermont
- Began migrating to Canada in the 1600s after many died from diseases brought by Europeans
- Many descendants live on two reservations in Québec, Canada, today

The White Mountains stand in northern New Hampshire. New England's highest point, Mount Washington, lies within them. Forests cover low mountains and rolling hills to the south. The Merrimack River begins in central New Hampshire. It flows south through hilly farmland. Islands dot Lake Winnipesaukee. Stretches of rocky and sandy shore line the Atlantic coast.

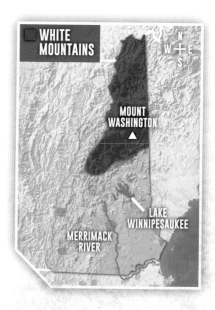

WHITE MOUNTAINS

N
W E
S

MOUNT WASHINGTON ▲

LAKE WINNIPESAUKEE

MERRIMACK RIVER

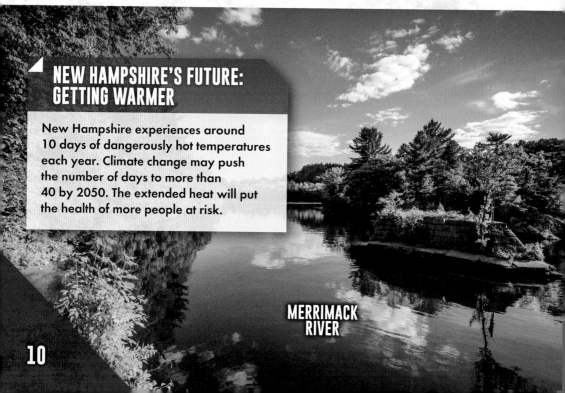

NEW HAMPSHIRE'S FUTURE: GETTING WARMER

New Hampshire experiences around 10 days of dangerously hot temperatures each year. Climate change may push the number of days to more than 40 by 2050. The extended heat will put the health of more people at risk.

MERRIMACK RIVER

MOUNT WASHINGTON

SPRING
HIGH: 44°F (7°C)
LOW: 25°F (-4°C)

SUMMER
HIGH: 67°F (19°C)
LOW: 48°F (9°C)

FALL
HIGH: 48°F (9°C)
LOW: 31°F (-1°C)

WINTER
HIGH: 25°F (-4°C)
LOW: 6°F (-14°C)

°F = degrees Fahrenheit
°C = degrees Celsius

New Hampshire is mild in summer and cold in winter. The mountains are cooler than the river valleys. Winter brings heavy snow. Wild winds blow on Mount Washington. Some of the world's highest wind speeds have been recorded there!

EASTERN PAINTED TURTLE

In New Hampshire's forests, white-tailed deer dash between trees. Purple finches sing from branches. Bobcats hunt squirrels and raccoons. Black bears search for berries and acorns. Moose chomp on birch and maple twigs. Swallowtail butterflies sip nectar from wildflowers.

Beavers bring down trees to dam rivers and streams. They create watery habitats for muskrats, turtles, and herons. Ospreys grab trout, bass, and salmon from New Hampshire's waters. Little brown bats swoop over wetlands to catch insects. Piping plovers nest on sandy beaches, while whales and dolphins swim offshore.

GREAT BLUE HERON

MOOSE

SHORT-BEAKED COMMON DOLPHIN

BLACK SWALLOWTAIL BUTTERFLY

PURPLE FINCH

Life Span: up to 14 years
Status: least concern

purple finch range =

LEAST CONCERN	NEAR THREATENED	VULNERABLE	ENDANGERED	CRITICALLY ENDANGERED	EXTINCT IN THE WILD	EXTINCT

13

About 9 in 10 New Hampshirites have European **ancestors**. Early settlers came from England, Scotland, and Ireland. Later, the state's industries drew other Europeans as well as French Canadians. Hispanic Americans and Asian Americans make up the next-largest groups. Smaller populations of Native American and Black or African American people also live in New Hampshire. Newcomers have arrived from India, Canada, China, the Dominican Republic, and Nepal.

PORTSMOUTH

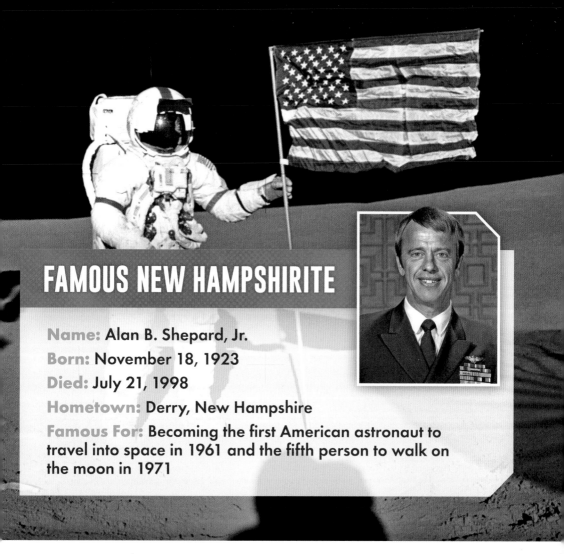

FAMOUS NEW HAMPSHIRITE

Name: Alan B. Shepard, Jr.

Born: November 18, 1923

Died: July 21, 1998

Hometown: Derry, New Hampshire

Famous For: Becoming the first American astronaut to travel into space in 1961 and the fifth person to walk on the moon in 1971

More than 1.3 million people call New Hampshire home. Around three out of five live in **urban** areas. The largest cities lie in the Merrimack Valley. The Manchester-Nashua **metropolitan** area has the largest population. **Rural** New Hampshirites live on farms and in small villages.

RURAL NEW HAMPSHIRE

The Abenaki once fished where Manchester stands on the Merrimack River. English and Scottish settlers made the site their home in the 1720s. One of the country's first **textile mills** was built in Manchester in 1805. The city's population grew. Today, Manchester is New Hampshire's largest city.

THE AMOSKEAG

The Amoskeag Manufacturing Company formed in 1831 in Manchester. The factory's mills turned cotton into cloth. The Amoskeag became one of the largest textile factories in the world.

Manchester's residents enjoy strolling the **Heritage** Trail along the Merrimack River. Lake Massabesic is great for boating. In winter, snow tubers hit the slopes at the McIntyre Ski Area. The SEE Science Center offers visitors hands-on fun as they explore exhibits. Crowds fill the Palace Theatre for stage performances.

PALACE THEATRE

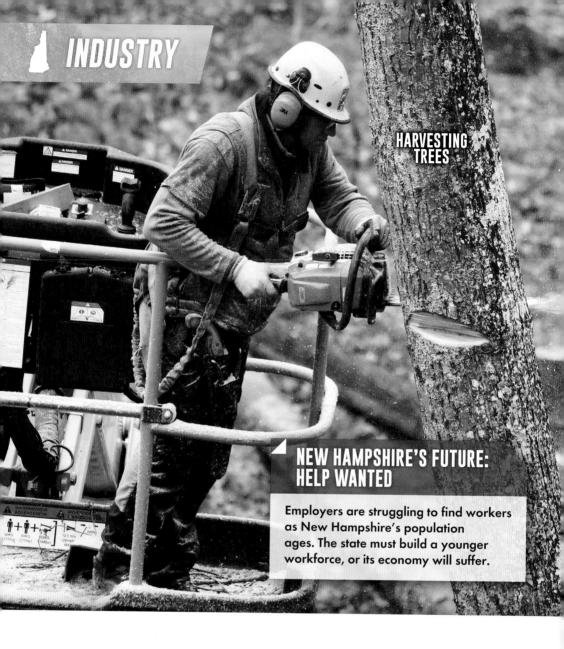

HARVESTING TREES

NEW HAMPSHIRE'S FUTURE: HELP WANTED

Employers are struggling to find workers as New Hampshire's population ages. The state must build a younger workforce, or its economy will suffer.

New Hampshire's **natural resources** support many jobs. In the forests, workers harvest trees for lumber and paper. Miners dig up sand, gravel, and granite throughout the state. Fishing crews haul in lobsters, cod, and herring off the coast. Top farm products include hay, apples, sweet corn, and maple sugar. Farmers also grow nursery plants in greenhouses.

Factory workers make electronics, machine parts, and medical equipment. The Portsmouth Naval Shipyard builds and maintains submarines. Most New Hampshirites have **service jobs**. They work in health care, education, and **tourism**.

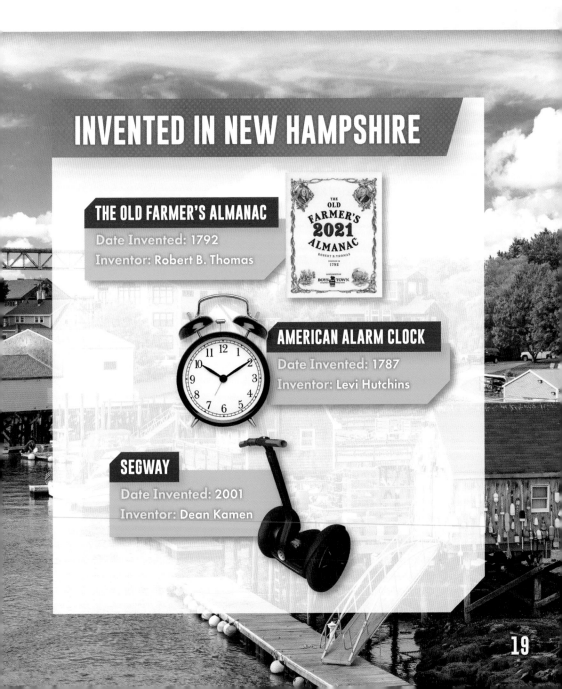

INVENTED IN NEW HAMPSHIRE

THE OLD FARMER'S ALMANAC

Date Invented: 1792

Inventor: Robert B. Thomas

AMERICAN ALARM CLOCK

Date Invented: 1787

Inventor: Levi Hutchins

SEGWAY

Date Invented: 2001

Inventor: Dean Kamen

CLAMBAKE

A POUTINE PARTY

Many New Hampshire restaurants serve poutine. The dish is usually made with french fries and cheese curds covered in gravy. But some restaurants put their own spin on this French-Canadian favorite.

New Hampshirites enjoy classic New England dishes. Lobster rolls and clam chowder are local favorites. Clambakes on the beach are a summer **tradition**. Clams, lobsters, potatoes, and corn are steamed in a pit. Cooks fry up bass pulled from the state's lakes. Hunters provide deer, moose, and other game for stews and sausages.

Apple cider is the state drink. It features in apple cider doughnuts. Sap collected from maple trees in spring is made into maple syrup. The syrup flavors maple walnut ice cream. This sweet treat is served at ice cream shops throughout the state.

LOBSTER ROLL

MAPLE WALNUT ICE CREAM

NEW HAMPSHIRE STEW

4 SERVINGS

Have an adult help you make this recipe.

INGREDIENTS

1/8 pound of salt pork cut into 1/4-inch cubes

2 tablespoons butter, divided

1 pound stew meat (beef or game), cubed

3 carrots sliced into 1-inch pieces

2 potatoes cut into eighths

1 onion, sliced

1 garlic clove, crushed

1 bay leaf

1 1/2 cups beef broth

1 1/2 cups vegetable broth

1 tablespoon flour

DIRECTIONS

1. In a medium-sized pot, brown the salt pork cubes in 1 tablespoon of butter until crisp.

2. Brown the cubes of stew meat in the remaining fat. Add the carrots, potatoes, onion, garlic, bay leaf, and broths.

3. Simmer covered for one hour or until the meat is tender.

4. Mix the remaining butter with flour until smooth. Stir into the stew. Cook 5 minutes longer to thicken. Remove the bay leaf before serving.

CAMPING

New Hampshirites make the most of the outdoors. In warm weather, the state parks fill with hikers and campers. Bikers pedal along mountain trails and country roads. Rushing rivers draw white-water rafters and kayakers. In winter, skiers and snowboarders whoosh down snow-covered slopes.

KAYAKING

Performances at the Barnstormers Theatre in Tamworth are a summer tradition. At the Children's Museum, visitors explore caves and discover dinosaurs. Sports fans cheer for the Fisher Cats baseball team. NASCAR racing thrills crowds at the New Hampshire Motor Speedway in Loudon.

NASCAR RACING

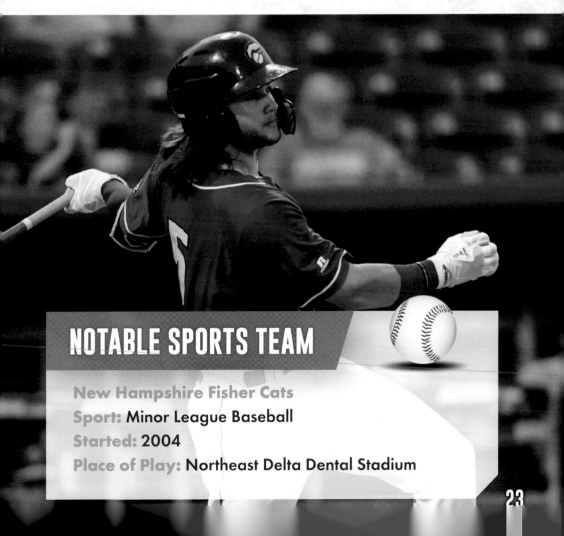

NOTABLE SPORTS TEAM

New Hampshire Fisher Cats
Sport: Minor League Baseball
Started: 2004
Place of Play: Northeast Delta Dental Stadium

New Hampshirites celebrate traditions throughout the year. Many brave the cold every February to celebrate the Newport Winter Carnival. They enjoy a parade, games, and midnight ice skating. In July and August, Portsmouth hosts the Prescott Park Arts Festival. A theater group performs a musical, and many musicians take the stage.

Colebrook's North Country Moose Festival is in August. It features a moose-calling contest, moose chili, and a barn dance. Costumed crowds enjoy the Keene Pumpkin Festival in October. They stroll among thousands of glowing jack-o-lanterns. New Hampshire's festivals bring communities together!

LUCKY DUCK

Every May, Jackson hosts the Wildquack Duck Race and Music Festival. A rubber ducky race is the main event. About 3,500 rubber duckies tumble down Jackson Falls. Prizes go to the winning entries!

KEENE PUMPKIN FESTIVAL

NEW HAMPSHIRE TIMELINE

1603
English explorer Martin Pring is likely the first European to explore New Hampshire

1788
New Hampshire becomes the ninth U.S. state

1853
New Hampshire native Franklin Pierce becomes the 14th U.S. president

1741
New Hampshire becomes an English colony

1808
Concord becomes New Hampshire's state capital

2012

New Hampshire is the first state where all officials elected to the U.S. Congress are women

2018

A powerful storm knocks out power for more than 63,000 people

2018

Chris Pappas is elected as the first openly gay person to represent New Hampshire in Congress

1918

The White Mountain National Forest is established in New Hampshire and Maine

2019

Governor Chris Sununu bans oil drilling off of New Hampshire's coast

Nickname: The Granite State

Motto: Live Free or Die

Date of Statehood: June 21, 1788 (the ninth state)

Capital City: Concord ★

Other Major Cities: Manchester, Nashua, Derry

Area: 9,349 square miles (24,214 square kilometers); New Hampshire is the 46th largest state.

Population

1,377,529

(2020)

STATE FLAG

New Hampshire's state flag was adopted in 1909. It features the state seal on a blue background. The seal includes the Revolutionary War ship *Raleigh* being built in Portsmouth. Golden leaves and nine golden stars circle the state seal. The stars show that New Hampshire was the ninth state.

INDUSTRY

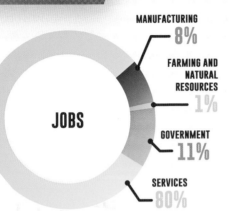

JOBS

MANUFACTURING
8%

FARMING AND
NATURAL
RESOURCES
1%

GOVERNMENT
11%

SERVICES
80%

Main Exports

aircraft
parts

machine
parts

medicines

cell phones

Natural Resources
forests, granite, sand, gravel

GOVERNMENT

Federal Government
2 REPRESENTATIVES | **2** SENATORS

4 ELECTORAL VOTES

USA

NH

State Government
400 REPRESENTATIVES | **24** SENATORS

STATE SYMBOLS

STATE BIRD
PURPLE FINCH

STATE ANIMAL
WHITE-TAILED DEER

STATE FLOWER
PURPLE LILAC

STATE TREE
WHITE BIRCH

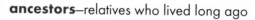
ancestors—relatives who lived long ago

gorge—a narrow canyon with steep walls

heritage—the traditions, achievements, and beliefs that are part of the history of a group of people

metropolitan—the combined city and suburban area

natural resources—materials in the earth that are taken out and used to make products or fuel

New England—an area in the northeastern United States that includes Maine, New Hampshire, Vermont, Massachusetts, Rhode Island, and Connecticut

Revolutionary War—the war from 1775 to 1783 in which the United States fought for independence from Great Britain

rural—related to the countryside

service jobs—jobs that perform tasks for people or businesses

settled—moved somewhere and made it home

textile mills—buildings with machines for processing woven or knitted cloth

tourism—the business of people traveling to visit other places

tradition—a custom, idea, or belief handed down from one generation to the next

urban—related to cities and city life

wigwam—a dome-shaped home made with bark or animal skins covering a structure of wooden poles

AT THE LIBRARY

Krull, Kathleen. *A Kids' Guide to the American Revolution*. New York, N.Y.: Harper, 2018.

Raum, Elizabeth. *Exploring the New Hampshire Colony*. North Mankato, Minn.: Capstone Press, 2017.

Yomtov, Nel. *New Hampshire*. New York, N.Y.: Children's Press, 2019.

ON THE WEB

FACTSURFER

Factsurfer.com gives you a safe, fun way to find more information.

1. Go to www.factsurfer.com.

2. Enter "New Hampshire" into the search box and click Q.

3. Select your book cover to see a list of related content.

INDEX

The images in this book are reproduced through the courtesy of: Christian Delbert, front cover, pp. 2-3; Steve Byland, pp. 3, 29 (purple finch); Daniel Dempster Photography/ Alamy, pp. 4-5; nobleIMAGES/ Alamy, p. 5 (Old Man on the Mountain); Wankun Jia, pp. 5 (Currier Museum of Art, Hampton Beach State Park), 14, 16 (top), 26 (bottom); KAZMAT, p. 5 (Mount Washington Cog Railway); Pernell Voyage, p. 5 (Strawbery Banke Museum); Ellen McKnight/ Alamy, p. 8; Jon Bilous, pp. 9, 11 (bottom), 27; Jon Bilous/ Alamy, p. 10; Denis Tangney Jr, p. 11 (top); Elizabeth Spencer, p. 12 (black swallowtail butterfly); David Byron Keener, p. 12 (eastern painted turtle); Joseph Scott Photography, p. 12 (great blue heron); Alicia Marvin, p. 12 (moose); Rob Jansen, p. 12 (short-beaked common dolphin); Ray Whittemore, p. 13; Universal Images Group North America LLC/ Alamy, pp. 15 (top), 16 (bottom); The Color Archives/ Alamy, p. 15 (middle); Albert Pego, p. 15 (bottom); Randy Duchaine/ Alamy, p. 17; Edward Fielding, p. 18; Patti McConville/ Alamy, p. 19 (Old Farmer's Almanac); JRP Studio, p. 19 (American alarm clock); photostar72, p. 19 (Segway); Sean Pavone, p. 19; Matthew Healey/ Alamy, p. 20 (top); FILMME, p. 20 (bottom); Marie Sonmez Photography, p. 21 (lobster roll); stockcreations, p. 21 (maple walnut ice cream); Anna Shepulova, p. 21 (stew top); Tatiana Volgutova, p. 21 (stew bottom); ajj_photos, p. 22 (top); EcoPhotography.com/ Alamy, p. 22 (bottom); Gridstone Media Group, p. 22 (top); Andrew Cline/ Alamy, p. 22 (middle); Naks Narodenko, p. 22 (bottom); ajt, p. 24; James Kirkikis, pp. 24-25; George Peter Alexander Healy/ Wikipedia, p. 26 (top); Sean Pavone, pp. 28-32; Michael Sean OLeary, p. 29 (white-tailed deer); photolinc, p. 29 (purple lilac); John A. Anderson, p. 29 (white birch); Volodymyr Burdiak, p. 31.